# The Truth About Fish and Chips

Contents





Written by Paul Mason

# A Favourite Dish

Do *you* like fish and chips? Fish and chips is one of the most popular meals in the world – especially in Great Britain and Australia!

But fish and chips has a secret story. There's a lot you might not know about this surprising dish. Where does it really come from?

This poster is from the 1920s. Fish and chips soon became popular in many countries.

Chips – but which is the best type of potato for making chips? Find out more on page 17.
Fish – flake is **traditional**. Find out more on page 10.

# Who Invented Chips?

Some people say that the Belgians invented chips in the 1700s. Some say it was the French. No one knows for sure!

# The Belgian Times

Some time in the 1700s

## Wonderful New Meal Ends Winter Woes!

### Mothers happy: "The kids have stopped moaning at last!"

It's been a long, freezing winter in Belgium. The river ice is so thick that fishing is impossible. If you're dreaming of a fishy meal, one local lady has a suggestion – try her new invention, "chips".

"The kids were moaning that they hadn't had fish for ages. They were really getting on my nerves. So I cut some potatoes into little fish shapes, and **fried** those. They loved them!"

By the twentieth century, "chips" were so popular that they were sold on the streets in Paris, France.

# The First Chips Recipe

If you want to try making chips the **original** way, try this recipe. Get an adult to help.

1

Peel a big potato and cut it into slices 1 cm thick.

2

Use a pastry cutter to cut out the fish shapes.

Boil the fish shapes in water for three minutes – no longer. Drain, and pat dry with paper towels.

Put the fish shapes into hot oil in a frying pan. Once they are brown underneath, turn them over to cook the other side.

When both sides are cooked, lift out the fish shapes and pat dry on paper towels.

# The First Fish-and-Chip Shop

Chips came from Belgium, or maybe France. The first fried-fish recipes came from Portugal. Suddenly fish and chips seem very **international**!

The first fish-and-chip shop was in Great Britain. It opened in the 1860s. Some people say it was opened by Joseph Malin in the East End of London. Others claim that John Lees, in Lancashire, beat him to it.

After the 1860s, fish-and-chip shops opened throughout Britain. There were even fish-and-chip carts!

Fish and chips always used to be served wrapped in old newspapers. In some countries, this is now **banned** because people think it is unhealthy.

# The Perfect Fish

Which is the best fish to have with chips? Most people pick cod. The trouble is, so many cod have been caught that there are not many left in the sea. This is called "over-fishing".

Today, many people prefer to eat something other than cod. They look for fish that tastes just as good, but has not been "over-fished".

## HERE ARE SOME YOU CAN TRY:

Pollack and coley taste a bit like cod. Halibut, a meaty fish like cod, is good if you don't like bones!

This blue label shows it's OK to buy a particular type of fish.

Fish is delicious and it is very good for your body and your brain! But for years fishermen have taken too many fish from the sea and in some places there are hardly any left. So now we have to make sure that we only buy fish that have been caught in the right parts of the sea, and that we never take too many.

**Hugh Fearnley-Whittingstall**
Food writer and **chef**

# Make Your Own Fish Fingers

Here's a recipe for yummy fish fingers from Hugh Fearnley-Whittingstall. Get an adult to help you make this!

## INGREDIENTS

- 250 g firm-fleshed fish (such as lemon sole or black bream), cut into 'fingers'
- 3 tbsp plain flour
- 2 eggs, **whisked**
- 100 g fine breadcrumbs
- Salt and pepper
- Some sunflower oil

1. Put the flour on a plate and **season** with salt and pepper. Put the whisked eggs in a bowl. Put the breadcrumbs on a plate.

2. Dip each finger of fish in the flour, then in the whisked egg, then in the breadcrumbs. Put them on a plate.

3. Get an adult to heat some sunflower oil in a frying pan over a medium heat. Fry the fish fingers (a few at a time) for about two minutes on each side until golden and crisp.

4. Drain on paper towels. Serve with a dip such as tomato sauce, mayonnaise, tartare sauce or yoghurt with garlic.

# How Fish and Chips Won Two World Wars

In 1914, and again in 1939, wars known as "World Wars" started in Europe. Few people know that a secret weapon helped Britain in both wars – fish and chips!

Meat and many other foods were **rationed**, but fish was not rationed.

TOP SECRET MEMO

From: The Prime Minister
To: Minister for Food

---

I am worried that people will be upset because we haven't won the war yet. Please make sure they have plenty of fish and chips to cheer them up.

The Prime Minister

---

IF IT WASN'T FOR GOOD OLD
**FISH AND CHIPS**
WE'D BE DOWN AND OUT BY NOW!

Posters like this were meant to remind people how lucky they were to have fish and chips – not how much they missed steak!

# From Peeled Potato to Perfect Chips

Chips from a fast-food shop are all the same shape and size. They have been made by machine.

# TO MAKE PERFECT CHIPS AT HOME

Don't forget to ask an adult to help you!

1. Choose the best potato! Many chefs use Coliban potatoes.

2. Choose the right fat. Beef fat is traditional, or you can use oil.

3. Cook the chips properly – three times! First, boil them for about three minutes. Then fry them at 120°C. Then fry them again, at 180°C.

**Hey presto – perfect chips!**

# Six Strange Facts About Potatoes

## 1

People often think Sir Francis Drake brought the first potatoes to Europe. It was actually Spanish sailors, in the late 1500s.

## 2

In 1995, a potato became the first food to be grown in Space.

## 3

The world's largest potato was grown in 2011. It weighed 5 kg – about the same as a small dog.

4

All parts of the potato plant are poisonous. Cooking potatoes makes them safe to eat.

5

During the Gold Rush in America in 1898, potatoes were worth as much as gold.

6

Potatoes are 80 per cent water. (So are human babies.)

# "Any Extras?"

Most people like to add extra flavours to their fish and chips. These are just a few of the most popular ones:

***Salt and vinegar***
often added to both fish and chips

***Mushy peas, gravy, or curry sauce***
popular in the north of England, Wales and Scotland

Tomato sauce or mayonnaise
usually added to the chips
Lemon juice
sometimes added
to the fish

# Fish and Chips Timeline

**8000–5000 BC**

Potatoes are grown by farmers in Peru, South America.

**1500s**

Potatoes are **exported** from South America to Europe.

*1860s*

The first fish-and-chip shop opens in Great Britain.

*1700s*

Chips first appear in Belgium and France.

Fried-fish recipes are brought to Britain from Portugal.

*1860s–today*

Fish-and-chip shops open in many countries.

The dish is still a favourite today!

# Glossary

| | |
|---|---|
| **banned** | not allowed |
| **chef** | person who cooks food as a job |
| **exported** | sent from one country to another |
| **fried** | cooked in hot oil or fat |
| **international** | to do with lots of different countries |
| **original** | first or earliest |
| **rationed** | given out in limited amounts |
| **season** | add extra flavour |
| **traditional** | done in the past |
| **whisked** | mixed using a fork |